AF261685

When They Call You the Villain

A Conversation Among Grandmothers

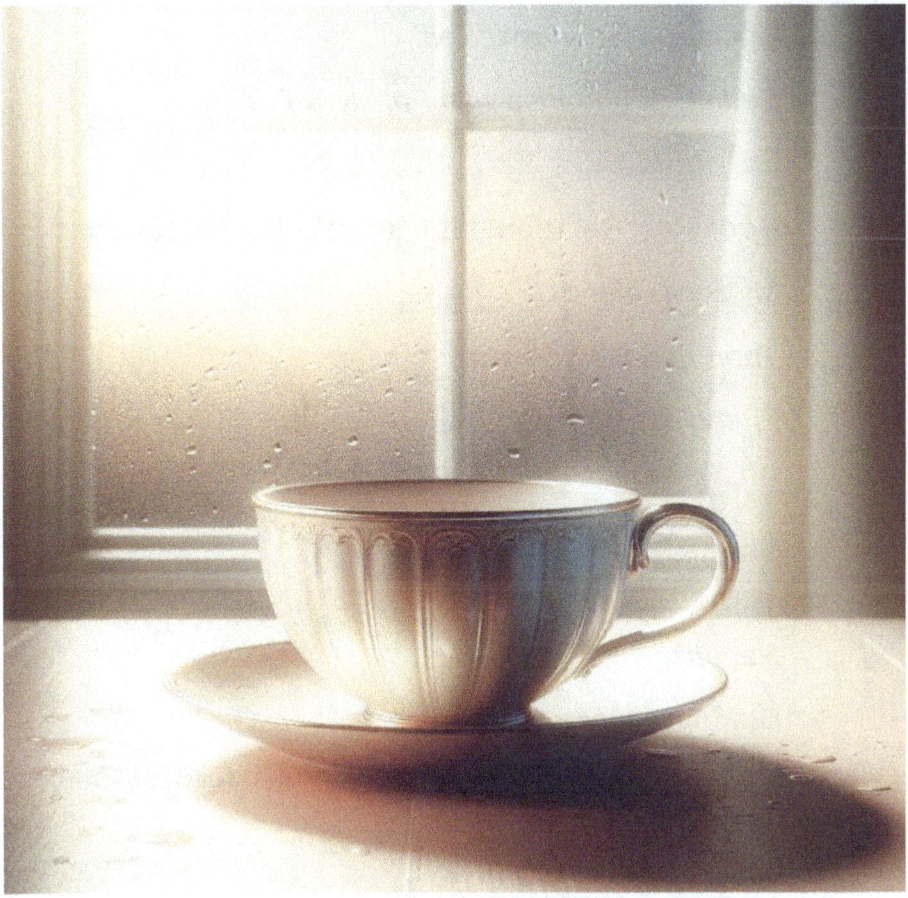

"Poetic, powerful, and deeply healing — this book will sit on your nightstand and in your soul."

Vgdawson

Books on Friendship, Relationships, and Personal Growth

Books on Personal Growth and Life Reflection

Unlocking Your Best Self

Setting Boundaries with Family & Friends

Books on Relationships and Personal Boundaries

My Best Friend

The Friendship Years

Friendless

Books for Readers Life After 50

The Truth about the Golden Years: What Aging Really Reveals

Discover More

Visit the author online for additional books, resources, and inspiration:

www.what2buynext.com

Published by
Second Season Press
Birmingham, Alabama
www.what2buynext.com
ISBN: 978-1-972518-16-8

Cataloging information is available from the Library of Congress.
Library of Congress Control Number: 2026912795
First Edition: 2026

This book is a work of nonfiction. The information presented is based on the author's experiences and research and is intended for educational and informational purposes only. The author and publisher disclaim any liability for any injury, damage, or loss resulting from the use of the information contained herein. Readers are encouraged to seek professional guidance when appropriate.

All brand names and product names referenced in this book are trademarks or registered trademarks of their respective owners. Their use is for identification purposes only and does not imply endorsement.

Printed in the United States of America

Disclaimer

The information and guidance in this book are based on the author's personal experiences, research, and perspectives. While the author has made every effort to provide accurate and helpful information, they cannot guarantee specific outcomes or results.

The stories and examples are illustrative and intended to provide a framework for your own reflection and growth. Your journey is unique, and your decisions should be based on your own personal circumstances, values, and, where appropriate, the guidance of licensed professionals.

The author and publisher disclaim any liability arising directly or indirectly from the use or application of any information contained in this book. If you require professional advice, you should seek the services of a competent professional.

Your well-being is the highest priority. Please take from this book what serves you and leave the rest.

Dedication

This book is dedicated to every woman who has ever been misunderstood, mislabeled, or misjudged for choosing peace.

To the grandmothers, mothers, daughters, and friends who found the courage to say, "No more," and meant it.

To those who chose quiet over chaos, healing over hostility, and peace over performance this book is your mirror.

And to my sisters in spirit who are learning that boundaries are love in practice this is for you.

Author's Note

Every word in this book was written from a place of truth not perfection, but healing.

These conversations among grandmothers began as whispers of my own story, reflections I have carried, and lessons I've learned from women who refused to stay broken just to keep others comfortable.

We've lived long enough to know that peace is not always quiet sometimes it comes after years of being misunderstood, misjudged, or mislabeled.

But even then, peace is worth it.

To every woman who has been called selfish for choosing herself, or difficult for setting boundaries, I hope these pages reminded you that you are not alone.

You are allowed to evolve.

You are allowed to rest.

You are allowed to choose yourself without guilt.

This book is not just about surviving misunderstanding, it's about reclaiming your right to live freely, love deeply, and rest fully.

You are not the villain. You are the evidence that healing changes everything.

With heartfelt gratitude,

—Vgdawson

Table of Contents

What Readers Are Saying

"This book feels like sitting at a kitchen table with women who understand you without judgment. Every page is truth and tenderness."
— Reader, 62

"I cried, I healed, I forgave myself. This book doesn't just speak to grandmothers — it speaks to every woman who's ever been misunderstood."
— Reader, 45

"Finally, someone said what I've been feeling for years. When They Call You the Villain gave me permission to rest."
— Reader, 58

"The wisdom in these pages reminded me of my own mother and grandmother. It's gentle, but it hits deep."
— Reader, 67

"Every chapter feels like a conversation I didn't know I needed. Beautifully written and soulfully healing."
— Reader, 39

What to Expect from This Book

Before you begin, let me speak to you woman to woman… heart to heart.

This is not a book you rush through.
This is a book you sit with.

Some pages may feel like a conversation you've been waiting to have your whole life.
Others may feel like someone finally put your silent thoughts into words.

And there may be moments when you have to pause not because it's too much, but because **it's too true.**

This Is Not a Book About Blame

You won't find finger-pointing here.
You won't find bitterness or harsh judgment.

This is not about tearing people down.
This is about **lifting yourself back up.**

We will talk about:

- Being misunderstood by family

- Being called selfish for setting boundaries

- Carrying responsibilities that were never meant to be yours alone

- Loving deeply… while slowly losing yourself

But we will talk about it with **honesty, grace, and wisdom.**

This Book Is a Conversation

Imagine sitting at a table with women who understand you.

Women who have:

- Raised children

- Loved beyond their limits

- Stayed longer than they should have

- Given more than they had

- And are now asking, *"What about me?"*

That's what this book is.

A conversation.
Not a lecture.
Not a set of rules.

You will hear stories, real-life moments, and quiet truths that feel familiar because they are.

You Will See Yourself in These Pages

You may see yourself in:

- The mother who gave everything and is still asked for more

- The grandmother who loves her family but is tired in ways no one sees

- The woman who finally says "no"… and is called the villain for it

- The friend who outgrew relationships that no longer felt safe

And when you do, I want you to know:

You are not alone.
And you are not wrong for feeling the way you feel.

Gentle Truths, Not Harsh Lessons

This book will not push you.
It will not demand that you change overnight.

Instead, it will offer:

- Soft wisdom

- Honest reflection

- Space to think

- Permission to feel

You will learn:

- The difference between love and obligation

- Why people sometimes blame you instead of facing themselves

- How to set boundaries without losing your heart

- How to choose peace without carrying guilt

You Will Be Asked to Reflect

Throughout this book, you will find moments where I ask you to pause.

To write.
To think.
To answer questions you may have avoided.

Not to judge yourself, but to understand yourself.

Because healing doesn't begin with answers.
It begins with honesty.

This Book Is for You If…

- You've ever been called selfish for choosing yourself

- You feel tired of being "the strong one"

- You love your family, but feel unseen or unappreciated

- You're learning that peace matters more than approval

- You're ready to live your life… not just support everyone else's

What You Will Leave With

By the time you finish this book, I hope you feel:

✓ **Lighter**
✓ **Clearer**
✓ **Seen**
✓ **Stronger in your truth**
✓ **More at peace with the choices you need to make**

Not because everything around you has changed…
but because something within you has.

A Final Word Before You Turn the Page

My friend…

You have carried a lot.
More than most people will ever understand.

This book is not here to tell you who you are.
It is here to remind you of who you've always been
a woman worthy of peace, respect, and a life that belongs to her.

Now… take a breath.

And let's begin.

A Conversation Among Grandmothers

There are stories that begin with laughter, and there are stories that begin with truth. This one begins with both.

I didn't write this book to defend the women who've been misunderstood. I wrote it to honor them.

The ones who were labeled cold because they stopped rescuing.

The ones who were called selfish because they finally rested.

The ones who were named "the villain" simply because they outgrew their silence.

This isn't a book about bitterness. It's about release.

It's about the kind of wisdom that only comes after years of loving, losing, forgiving, and finally choosing peace.

Four grandmothers. Four stories. One table filled with tea, truth, and tenderness.

They sit together, not to judge or advise, but to reflect to say the things they once swallowed to keep the peace.

Each chapter is a conversation a moment where wisdom meets weariness, and grace meets growth.

By the end, you may find pieces of yourself in their stories.

You may remember a mother, a sister, or a version of you who gave too much trying to be loved enough.

You may even feel the peace that comes when you stop explaining your healing to those who never earned your pain.

This book is not about becoming someone new, it's about coming home to who you've always been.

"They may call you the villain,

but peace will call you free."

Welcome to the table.

Let's begin.

Chapter 1 – Are We the Villains Now?

A Conversation Among Grandmothers

The Gathering

It was late afternoon when the four of them arrived at my house no make-up, no rushing, no pretending. Just tired hearts and soft voices. The kind of tired that sleep can't fix. The kind of tired that comes from loving too hard, giving too long, and being told it still wasn't enough.

The tea kettle had just stopped whistling. Cups were laid out on the oak table I've had since my children were young. These women my friends for over forty years sat down slowly, like the weight of their lives had finally caught up with their bones. We are all grandmothers now. Different ages. Different stories. But we have one thing in common, we were the ones who held everything and everyone together. And somehow, we became the ones they now blame.

Lynn was the first to speak. She looked at me with watery eyes and whispered, "When did we become the bad guys in our own families?"

No one laughed. No one dismissed it. Because the truth of that question sat heavy in all of us.

The Question No One Says Out Loud

"I mean…" she continued, staring into her cup, "I gave my whole life to my kids. I missed sleep, gave up dreams, worked two jobs… and now that I finally say 'no' to something, they call me selfish. How?"

Silence. The kind that hurts.

"They're not kids anymore," I said softly. "But some people don't grow out of needing a hero. And when the hero gets tired, they call her the villain."

They all looked at me. Not because I had the perfect answer, but because I wasn't afraid to say the truth out loud.

Real Conversation, Real Hurt

Monica: "My daughter said I 'abandoned her' because I told her I can't babysit every weekend. I'm 64. My knees hurt. But when I said I needed rest, she told me I 'don't care about family anymore.'"

Sandra: "My son only calls when he needs money. Last week, I told him I couldn't help this time. He said, 'Wow, you got cold in your old age.' Cold. Can you believe that?"

Lynn: "Mine said, 'You were never really there for me emotionally.' After all I did. The sacrifices. The nights I cried while holding everything together. And now I'm… the villain?"

I listened. And then I spoke what needed to be said.

Why They Blame Us (Even When We Gave Everything)

"It's not that they don't remember what we did for them," I said. "It's that remembering would make them feel guilty. And guilt is heavy. So instead of carrying it, they hand it to us."

Blame is easier than accountability.

Calling you selfish is easier than admitting they became dependent.

Telling others you 'changed' is easier than admitting you finally set boundaries.

Some people can't look in the mirror and face the truth of what they've taken. So they rewrite the story and hand you the role of the villain.

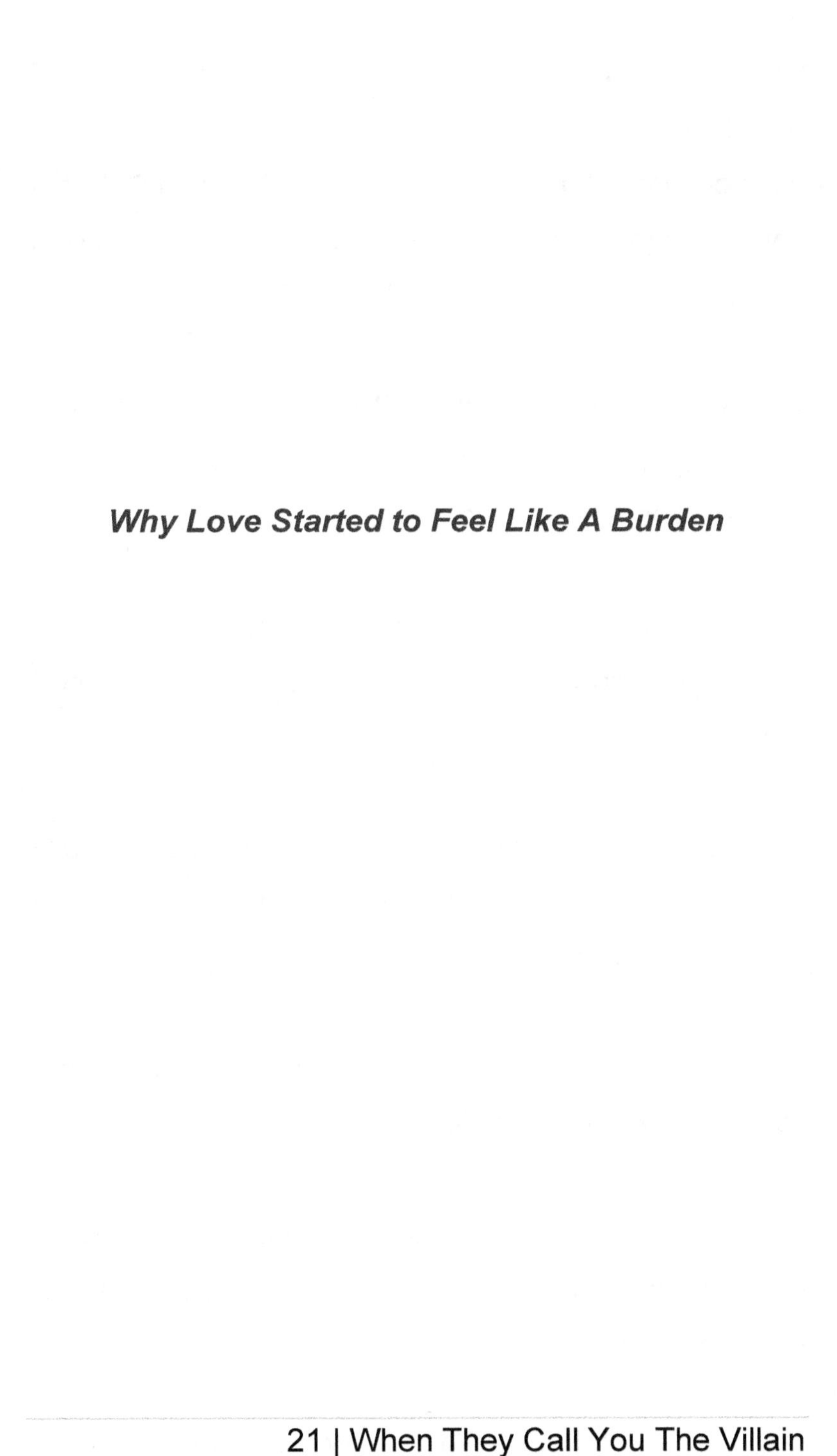

Why Love Started to Feel Like A Burden

Why Do They Blame Us? (The Gentle Truth Behind the Hurt)

"Our children don't see themselves as villains," I said softly, "because most of the time, they're not trying to hurt us. They're trying not to feel guilty."

Guilt is a powerful emotion. It makes people feel like they owe, like they didn't do enough, like they failed the woman who never failed them.

And instead of facing that truth? They push it away. Sometimes right onto the very person who carried them.

They say, "You're selfish now," when what they really mean is, "I don't like that you're no longer doing everything for me."

They say, "You've changed," because you no longer say yes to what drains you.

They call you "cold," "distant," or "hard," because for the first time in your life, you stopped choosing pain in the name of love.

"It's easier for them to say we're the problem," I said, "than to admit they got comfortable with us sacrificing ourselves."

No one argued. They just sipped their tea and blinked away tears.

When Love Slowly Becomes Obligation

It doesn't happen overnight.

Love turns into obligation quietly; the same way daylight turns into dusk. No loud announcement. Just a steady fading.

It begins with small things:

"Mom, can you watch the baby for a few hours?"

"Can I borrow some money until Friday?"

"Can you help me with this one last thing?"

And because we're mothers, we do it. Gladly.

But then… Friday never comes. The baby becomes your responsibility every weekend. The one last thing becomes everything.

And soon, you're not being asked. You're being expected.

That's the moment love shifts from freely given to quietly demanded.

"Mom, You're All He Has"

Sandra put her hands in her lap and said, "Can I tell you something I haven't told anyone?"

We nodded.

"My daughter dropped her two kids off at my house saying she just needed a break. That was nine months ago."
We listened silently.
"She told me, 'Mom, you're all they have. You're the only stable one.' And I believed her. I love my grandbabies. But I'm tired. I raised my kids. I thought this season of life would be gentler."

She swallowed hard.

"Last week, I told her I needed help. That I couldn't keep doing this alone. And do you know what she said? 'You're selfish. You love your freedom more than your family.'"

Her voice broke.

"I gave up my freedom to raise her. And now I'm selfish because I want to keep what little is left of my life?"

No one spoke.

I reached across the table and put my hand over hers.

"You're not selfish," I said. "You're human. You're a woman who loved so hard, everyone assumed you didn't need loving back."

Gentle Wisdom

"When people depend on your strength for too long, they forget it's possible for you to break."

When Guilt Is Handed to the Ones Who Gave Everything

"You Make Me Feel Like a Bad Daughter"

Monica stared at the steam rising from her cup. "You know what hurts?" she said. "It's not what they ask us to do. It's what they say when we can't do it anymore."

We listened.

"My daughter called me last week. She said she wanted to go out of town for a friend's trip. Could I watch the boys? I said, 'Baby, I love them. But I have a doctor's appointment, and my back's been hurting. I need rest.'"

She exhaled slowly.

"And do you know what she said? 'You make me feel like a bad daughter for asking. You always make me feel guilty when I need you.'"

Her voice cracked.

"All I said was 'I can't this time.' Not 'never.' Just not this time. And it turned into me being the reason she felt guilty."

I reached over, squeezed her hand.

"It's not your job to protect her from guilt," I said softly. "Sometimes guilt is the sign that they're finally seeing how much you've carried. And that's not cruelty that's truth staring back at them."

Why They Hand Us Their Guilt
Guilt is uncomfortable. It forces a person to confront reality:

📌 **Maybe I've asked for too much.**

📌 **Maybe I've taken her for granted.**

📌 **Maybe I forgot she has a life too.**

But instead of sitting with that truth — they try to escape it.
And how do they escape it? By giving it to you.
They say:
"You're making me feel bad."
"You're being dramatic."
"You're acting brand new."
"You don't care about family anymore."

But what they really mean is:

"I don't like how it feels when you stop being who I needed you to be."

When You're Tired of Being the Strong One
"I didn't tell y'all this," Lynn said softly, "but last month I told my son I couldn't co-sign his apartment lease."

We all looked at her. Lynn rarely opens up first.

"He's 32. Has a good job. But bad credit from years of messing up. And he said, 'Ma, I need you.' And I told him, 'Son, I love you, but I can't be your safety net forever.'"

She blinked back tears.

"He didn't speak to me for two weeks. Then I heard from my niece he told the family I 'turned my back on him when he needed me most.' Me; his mother. After everything. I didn't turn my back. I just stopped carrying a grown man on my shoulders."
Not one of us disagreed.

What I Told Them

I took a breath and said softly, "Listen to me. Every one of you."

They looked up.

"You are not cold. You are not selfish. You are not the villain."

"You are tired because you have given more love than most people will ever understand."

"You are asking for peace, not power. Rest, not revenge. Boundaries do not make you heartless. They make you honest."

"And sometimes," I said, "the people who depended on your silence will call you cruel the moment you start telling your truth."

And Then — The Quietest Question

Sandra wiped her eyes. "So what do we do?

Do we keep giving until there's nothing left?

Or do we pull back and let them call us heartless?"

"Neither," I said. "We don't become ruthless. But we don't live toothless either."

"We become wise."

Ruthless or Toothless? Finding the Middle Ground

"Do We Have to Be Ruthless to Be Respected?"

Sandra leaned forward. "So what then? Because I'm telling you right now, I'm tired of being quiet. Sometimes I want to say, 'Figure it out yourself. I owe you nothing.'"

The table fell silent.

Then Monica spoke softly, "I don't want to be cold like that. But I also don't want to keep being walked on. Why does it feel like we only have two options — be a doormat or be heartless?"

They turned to me. Not because I had all the answers, but because I had survived these questions before they did.

My Answer — The Balance of Wisdom

"You don't have to be ruthless," I said.

"But you also don't have to be toothless."

They waited.

"Ruthless is when love becomes anger. Toothless is when love becomes self-abandonment. Wisdom lives in the middle. It says: I can love you and still choose me. I can give, but not at the expense of my soul."

They nodded slowly.

The Honest Conversation That Followed

Me: "We were raised to believe good mothers give everything. That good women stay quiet. But look where that left us; exhausted, resentful, sick in our bodies, quiet in our suffering. That is not love. That is martyrdom."

Lynn: "But they'll still call us selfish…"

Me: "Let them. Do you know what selfish actually means? It means you stopped dying so other people could live comfortably."

Silence. Then soft laughter; the kind that comes with truth and relief.

Gentle Wisdom (Friend to Friend)

There's a difference between:

____

ENABLING vs. EMPOWERING

____

ENABLING:

• I do everything for them, even when they can do it themselves.

• I feel responsible for their happiness, emotions, or comfort.

• I say "yes" to avoid guilt, conflict, or being called selfish.

• I love them more than I love myself.

EMPOWERING:

• I help them learn to stand on their own feet.

• I support their emotions, but I don't carry them.

• I say "no" when my peace, health, or spirit is at risk.

• I love them and I love myself too.

"I Love Them… But I'm Losing Myself"

"I need to say something," Monica whispered.

We leaned in.

"My son lives with me. He's 38. Doesn't help with bills. Leaves dishes in the sink. Sleeps until noon. And when I ask him to help, he says, 'Why are you always on me? This is my home too.'"

Her voice trembled.

"And I love him… but I'm starting to resent him."

I reached out and placed my hand on hers.

"Resentment is what grows where boundaries should've been," I said gently. "You don't push him out in anger. You guide him toward adulthood with love, but also with limits."

She wiped a tear. "So I can love him and still say, 'This isn't working'?"

"Yes," I said. "Because love without boundaries is not love. It's imprisonment for both of you."

A Moment of Truth

This wasn't just about our children.

It was about us women who spent decades being everything for everyone.

And now, in this season of grandmotherhood, we are asking a different question:

"When do I get to live, too?"

When Did We Stop Living Our Own Lives?

The room grew quiet. Not the quiet of discomfort, but the kind that follows truth heavy, but freeing.

Sandra leaned back in her chair, ran her finger around the rim of her mug, and asked softly:

"When did our lives stop belonging to us?"

It wasn't an accusation. It wasn't anger. It was grief.

The Silent Pause of a Life on Hold

We all felt it.

At some point, without a sound, without a warning, we stopped living for ourselves.

We became:

The mother who never sat down.

The grandmother who always said, "Of course, baby, bring them over."

The peacemaker, the provider, the one everyone called before they called God.

We love our families. That is not in question. But somewhere along the way, love turned into duty, and duty turned into identity.

And now?

Now we are in our 50s, 60s, even 70s — and our phones still ring with "Can you…?" instead of "How are you?"

A Moment of Honesty

Monica: "I thought once my kids were grown, I'd finally rest."

Lynn: "I thought I'd travel, maybe fall in love again, take a pottery class."

Sandra (whispers): "I thought I'd finally learn who I am outside of being 'Mom.'"

Me: "So what happened?"

They didn't answer. They just looked tired.

The Guilt That Keeps Us from Choosing Ourselves

Choosing yourself after a lifetime of choosing others…
feels wrong at first.
It feels like betrayal.
It feels like sin.

Why? Because for years, we were taught:

Good mothers give everything.

Good grandmothers never say no.

Good women suffer with a smile.

But here's what I told them and what I'll tell you:

Living a life of constant sacrifice is not love; it is slow self-erasure.
And God, nor love, ever asked us to disappear.

The Plane Ticket She Never Bought
"I got an email from a travel group," Lynn said. "Women our age going to Italy — vineyards, museums, slow mornings with coffee. I wanted to go so badly."

She smiled sadly.

"But when I mentioned it to my daughter, she said, 'Must be nice to go on vacation when I'm here struggling with the kids and bills.'"

She swallowed hard. "I closed the email and never opened it again."

I looked her in the eye.
"You deserve to see Italy," I said gently.

"You deserve mornings where nobody needs you."

"You deserve to be more than someone else's solution."

Her eyes filled, but she nodded.

Truth I Spoke to All of Us

"We are not abandoning them by choosing ourselves sometimes."

"We are showing them what healthy looks like in a woman who has given enough."

"We are not villains. We are women who are finally remembering we exist, too."

What About Us?

The teacups were nearly empty. The sun was sliding low behind the trees. But nobody moved to leave. There was still something heavy in the room does not anger, not regret but the quiet ache of women finally admitting:

"I want more for myself. And I don't want to apologize for it anymore."

I leaned forward.

"Before we go any further," I said, "I want each of you and anyone reading this to answer honestly. Not as a mother, not as a grandmother, not as someone people depend on but as a woman."

If You're Brave Enough to Answer

Write these gently. Cry if you need to. This is for you.

When was the last time someone asked how you were without needing anything from you?

When was the last time you did something just for yourself?

(And did you enjoy it… or feel guilty the whole time?)

What parts of your life feel heavy right now? Who or what is making you feel responsible for their happiness?

If you stopped being "the strong one," who would you be?

What dream, trip, hobby, or rest have you postponed because someone else needed you?

What is one small boundary your heart is begging you to set?

They Finally Answer

Sandra (whispering): "I don't even know what I like anymore."

Monica: "I feel guilty resting. Like I have to earn it."

Lynn: "Sometimes I want to turn my phone off and just be unreachable. But I'm scared they'll hate me for it."

Me (softly): "They might not understand at first. But peace was never meant to be approved by everyone. Sometimes it's chosen quietly, bravely, and alone."

Gentle Affirmations – Read These Slowly

I am allowed to choose peace without being called selfish.

I am not a villain for saying "no" to what hurts me.

I was never meant to be everyone's solution.

Rest is not a reward; it is a right.

I love my family, and I also choose to love myself.

Saying "no" to others is sometimes saying "yes" to my healing.

I can be soft and still have boundaries.

I am not abandoning them; I am returning to myself.

The room stayed quiet. But it wasn't heavy anymore. There was relief. Validation. Something like... breathing again.

I looked at them at the lines on their faces, the stories in their hands.

"We are not done learning how to live," I said. "And we are not too old to begin again."

We Can Love Them Without Losing Ourselves

The sky had turned a soft, dusky blue. Streetlights had begun to glow outside the window. No one reached for their keys. No one stood to go. We were exactly where we needed to be heard.

Sandra broke the silence.

"Do you think they'll ever understand?"

I looked at her for a moment, then answered honestly.

"Maybe. Maybe not. Understanding isn't guaranteed. But peace? Peace is still possible even if they never admit what they did or how much you gave."

"I Didn't Leave Because I Stopped Loving Them…"
"I need to tell you something I've never said out loud," I said quietly.

They turned to me.

"You all know I stopped going to every family event a few years ago. Sunday dinners. Last-minute babysitting.

The constant calls 'Can you come?' 'Can you help?'"

I paused.

"What I didn't tell you was that it broke me before it healed me."

I swallowed hard.

"I didn't leave because I stopped loving them. I stepped back because I couldn't keep losing myself to keep everyone else comfortable. I was starting to forget who I was when no one needed me."

Their eyes glistened because they understood.

"I still love my family. I still help. But now, I help from health, not guilt. I give from fullness, not exhaustion. And that," I said, "is the difference between love and self-erasure."

Wisdom from the Table

I leaned in slightly and said, "Let me be clear choosing peace doesn't make you the villain. Sometimes it makes you the first honest person in a long line of people who pretended everything was fine."

"And sometimes, the people who loved you most will call you selfish simply because you stopped dying for them."

"But life is not meant to be a slow disappearance. At this age grandmother, great-grandmother, widow, wife, whatever we are this is not the end of something. This is the beginning of finally living with truth."

Before you turn the page, breathe.

Ask yourself:

What have I been carrying that is no longer mine to hold?

Who have I been trying to save, and in the process, have I stopped saving myself?

If I weren't afraid of being called selfish, what would I choose today?

Write your answers. Not to justify yourself to anyone but to free yourself.

As the evening ended, I said softly:

"We've talked about us, our exhaustion, our boundaries, our desire for peace. But next time… let's talk about our children. Not as babies we raised, but as adults who still need us in ways that break us and bind us."

"Because love is beautiful. But love without boundaries becomes a beautiful prison."

Between "The Beginning of Becoming the Villain" and "The Mother Wound"

Sit with this for a moment before you turn the page.

You've just spoken your first truth, the one that begins it all:

That sometimes being misunderstood isn't about what you did wrong, but about what you finally did right.

You've taken your first step away from guilt and closer to grace.

And now, you stand at the edge of understanding your story, not the one they told about you, but the one your soul remembers.

Before you enter the next chapter, breathe deeply.

This is where the healing begins ,where the child inside you meets the woman you've become, and together, they stop apologizing for surviving.

You do not have to explain your becoming.

You only have to honor it.

"I am not broken for needing peace.

I am brave for choosing it."

Carry that truth with you.

The next pages will ask you to look back not to live there, but to understand why you had to leave.

Chapter 2 – When Love Becomes Obligation: Mothers, Daughters & Unspoken Guilt

The Heavy Kind of Love

The next time we gathered around my table, the conversation didn't start with laughter or soft memories of long ago. It started with a sigh.

A heavy one.

The kind a mother makes when she holds both love and exhaustion in the same breath.

Sandra put her hands around her cup, warming them, and whispered:

"Why does it feel like being a mother never ends? Not the love, I don't ever want that to end. But the needing. The taking. The guilt. When does that part stop?"

No one rushed to answer.

Because it was a real question. And a brave one.

The Transition Nobody Talks About

Becoming a mother is talked about endlessly.

Becoming a grandmother is celebrated with balloons and baby showers.

But what no one talks about is the in-between that quiet, painful shift when:

Your children are adults…

But still expect you to fix, help, rescue, or finance their lives.

You say "no" and suddenly, you're cold, distant, or "not like you used to be."

It's not the diapers or the midnight feedings that break us in this season.

It's the unspoken expectation that we must keep saving them no matter what it costs us.

At the Table Again

Monica: "My daughter told me, 'You're my mother, you're supposed to help.' I said, 'Baby, I've been helping for 38 years.' She hung up on me."

Lynn: "My son said, 'You act like you don't need family anymore.' No. I just don't want to be the only one holding it up."

Sandra: "When I help them, I'm loved. When I say I can't… I'm the selfish one."

They looked at me.

"So what do we do?" Monica asked.

My Answer — The Truth Wrapped in Love

"You don't stop loving them," I said.
"But you stop believing that love means saving them."

They waited quietly.

"Love is not supposed to drain us. Motherhood is not a life sentence of self-sacrifice."

They leaned in.

"Your adult children are not your assignment. They are your legacy. And a legacy should be loved; not carried on your back."

Why Children Become Dependent (Even When They're Grown)

I told them gently not as a critic, but as someone who had lived it:

Sometimes our adult children struggle because:

✓ They were never taught how to do life without us stepping in.

✓ We rescued them so often that consequences never taught them anything.

✓ Our love blurred into enabling and now they don't know the difference.

✓ We replaced boundaries with guilt. They replaced accountability with blame.

And when we finally say "no," they feel abandoned not because we abandoned them, but because we stopped abandoning ourselves.

When Love Becomes Obligation

"You Owe Me Because You're My Mother"

Monica was the first to speak.

She rubbed her palms together the way she does when she's hurting but trying not to cry. "I need to tell y'all something… something that broke me more than I expected."

We stayed quiet. We knew that tone.

"My daughter called last week. She said her rent was short again. She needed six hundred dollars. I told her, 'Baby, I just paid my car insurance, I don't have it right now.'"

The table stayed still.

"And do you know what she said? She said, 'You're my mother. You're supposed to help me. You owe me that much after everything.'"

Her voice cracked on the word "owe."

The Wound No One Sees

"It's that word," she whispered. "Owe. Like my love was a debt I never finish paying."

I reached for her hand.

"Love is not a loan. Motherhood is not a contract," I said softly.

"You do not owe your children your peace, your sleep, your retirement, or your last breath just because you carried them."

Across the table, Sandra let out a quiet, broken, "Amen."

Why This Hurts So Deeply

When a child, even a grown one, says, "You owe me," it does three things to a mother's heart:

It erases everything we already gave.

The sleepless nights. The prayers. The bills paid. The dreams postponed. All of it gone in one sentence.

It turns love into a transaction.

"If you don't give me what I want, then you don't really love me."

It makes us question ourselves.

Am I a bad mother? Did I not give enough? Is this my fault?

But here is the truth I want you and every reader to hear:

A good mother gives from love, not obligation.

A grown child receives with gratitude, not entitlement.

The Honest Response

Monica: "I wanted to yell. I wanted to scream, 'I've given you my life!' But I didn't. I just sat there… quiet."

Me: "You didn't respond because you were never meant to defend your motherhood. You know what you gave. God knows. Your body knows. Your memories know."

Sandra: "So what do we do?"

Me: "We stop giving from guilt. We start giving from health. We stop carrying what they are old enough to carry themselves."

Ask yourself—

Have I ever been made to feel guilty for choosing myself?

When was the last time I gave something I didn't have to give?

What would loving my children with boundaries not burn out look like?

When Love Becomes Obligation

"But You're the Only One I Have"

Lynn hadn't said much since we sat down. She just listened, nodding slowly, her hands wrapped around a mug that had long gone cold.

When she finally spoke, her voice was tired not shaky, not angry, just tired in that deep, soul-level way.

"I love my son," she said. "Y'all know that. But I am drowning in being his 'only person.'"

The Story She Told Us

"My son calls me every day. Not to say hello. Not to check on me. But because he needs something money, advice, childcare, validation."

She took a slow breath.

"If I don't answer the phone, he sends three messages:

'Mom?'

'Are you okay?'

'Why are you ignoring me?'"

We stayed silent.

"But the moment I say I'm tired, I can't talk right now, I need rest..."

He says the same thing every time:

'Wow. You're all I have. And even you don't want me.'"

Emotional Manipulation in Soft Clothing

He didn't scream.

He didn't curse.

He didn't threaten to never speak to her again.

He simply laid his pain at her feet… and walked away, leaving her to carry both.

That's the hardest kind of guilt

The quiet kind.

The emotional kind.

The kind that sounds like love but feels like pressure.

Why This Happens

When adult children haven't developed the emotional tools to cope with life on their own, they often "borrow strength" from their mothers.

But if that borrowing turns into dependence, and dependence goes on for too long… the child begins to believe that connection is survival and any boundary becomes betrayal.

So when the mother pulls back, even gently, the child hears:

"You don't love me anymore."

Should that be true? No.

But emotionally

they feel abandoned.

they feel unimportant.

they feel exposed to life without a shield.

And because pain needs somewhere to go they send it back to the safest person they know.

Their mother.

What I Told Lynn

I placed my hand over hers.

"You were never meant to be somebody's only lifeline," I said softly.

"Love is sacred, but it is not supposed to replace personal responsibility."

She looked at me with tired, grateful eyes.

"You are allowed to say, 'I love you deeply, but I cannot be your everything.'"

Ask yourself gently:

Do I feel guilty when I don't answer the phone?

Have I ever felt responsible for someone else's emotional stability?

Do I confuse love with rescuing?

What would it sound like if I said, "I love you, but I need space"?

When Gratitude Turns Into Expectation

The room was quiet again. Not because there was nothing left to say, but because each of us was thinking about the same thing:

We don't mind loving. What we mind is being expected to love without limits.

Sandra broke the silence.

"You're Lucky to Have Grandkids. Why Do You Complain?"

"I was talking to my niece," Sandra said quietly, "and I told her I was tired just tired from watching my grandbabies four days a week while my daughter works and goes out with her friends."

"She looked me dead in my face and said, 'Auntie, at least your grandkids want to be around you. Some people don't have that. You shouldn't complain.'"

Sandra's voice trembled not with anger, but with hurt.

"Do you know what that did to me? It shut my mouth. It told me I wasn't allowed to be tired. That love meant silence. That if I spoke up, I was ungrateful."

The Invisible Weight Grandmothers Carry

This is what people don't see:

We aren't complaining about our grandchildren.

We are grieving our exhaustion.

We are grieving the version of ourselves we never got to become.

We are grieving the rest we keep postponing.

Being a grandmother is a blessing. But being treated like a built-in babysitter, nurse, ATM, counselor, and emergency contact without rest or recognition hurts.

Emotional Truth: Love and Exhaustion Can Exist Together

It is possible to:

✓ **Love your grandkids with your whole heart…**

✓ **And still need a day when no one calls your name.**

You can:

✓ **Be grateful for family…**

✓ **And still want quiet mornings where nobody needs anything from you.**

We must stop believing exhaustion cancels love.

Conversation Around the Table

Lynn: "They say, 'You always complain.' But they don't see the nights I can't sleep because my back hurts from lifting toddlers."

Monica: "They say, 'You're blessed.' But blessings shouldn't break your spirit."

Me: "You are blessed. But you are also tired. And both things can be true."

Soft Wisdom I Shared

"There is a difference between helping and becoming the solution to their every crisis."

"A good grandmother gives love, not her entire body, health, savings, and soul."

"And if they call you selfish for setting limits, it doesn't mean you're selfish it means they were used to your sacrifice."

Write honestly:

What do I love about being a mother or grandmother?

What parts of it are draining me but I'm scared to say out loud?

Who assumes I'll always be available? How does that make me feel?

What is one boundary my future peace is begging me to set?

The Cost of Always Being the Strong One

The house had grown quiet. Not the silence of distance, but of women thinking… women remembering.

I looked at the faces around the table, women who've held secrets, sacrifices, whole families together. Women who survived heartbreak, death, betrayal, and kept smiling so their children would feel safe.

And it hit me:

We became "the strong ones" because we had no other choice.

But now they expect strength from us like it costs nothing.

"If You Don't Help Me, I'll Lose Everything"

"My son called me at 11 p.m.," Monica said softly. "He was in a panic. He said rent was due tomorrow, and if he didn't pay, he'd be evicted. And then he said the words I hate the most—"

She paused. We all leaned in.

"If you don't help me… I'll lose everything. Don't you care?"

"I sat there," she whispered, "holding the phone, staring at my checking account. I had the money, but it was my light bill. My medication. My groceries for the month."

"So I sent it anyway."

Her voice broke.

"And he didn't say thank you. He just said, 'I knew you wouldn't let me fall.'"

Why This Isn't Just About Money

This isn't about $600 for rent. Or babysitting. Or rides to work.

This is about:

Being taken for granted.

Being told your love is an obligation.

Being expected to suffer quietly because "that's what mothers do."

It's about love turning into debt and debt turning into resentment.

Telling the Truth Out Loud

Sandra: "We don't get to be weak. If we cry, people say we're dramatic."

Lynn: "If we say no, we're selfish. If we keep saying yes, we're empty."

Me: "That's because the world applauds our strength but never asks about the cost."

Gentle Truth I Shared with Them

"Being strong was never the problem.

The problem is they forgot we are also human."

"You can love your children and still refuse to destroy yourself to save them."

"Saving someone every time they fail doesn't teach them love, it teaches them dependency."

"We are not God. We are not made of magic. We are women, with bodies that ache and hearts that sometimes want to rest."

Write honestly; no guilt, no judgment:

What does being 'the strong one' cost me emotionally? Physically? Spiritually?

Who have I saved so many times that they never learned to save themselves?

What would happen if I didn't answer the phone every time they called?

What do I need that I keep telling myself I can live without?

Affirmations

I am allowed to be tired.

I am allowed to have limits.

I am not a bad mother for choosing rest.

I can love deeply without losing myself completely.

I have given enough to feel worthy of peace.

I release the belief that I must break to prove my love.

When Love Needs Boundaries Too

The room had grown still. Not because we ran out of things to say; but because we finally started telling the truth.
Not the softened truth we tell our children.
Not the quiet truth we whisper to God when the house is dark.
But the kind of truth we only tell in safe company, with women who've lived it too.

"So What Does Love Look Like Now?"
Sandra asked it quietly, almost like a child asking permission.

"If we're not supposed to keep giving until we're empty," she said, "then what does love look like now? Now that we're in this stage of life; mothers, grandmothers… tired, but still trying?"

I looked at her. I thought for a moment. And I said:
"Love, at our age, should not look like martyrdom.
Love should look like balance.
Like choices.
Like helping because we want to not because we're scared not to."

Boundaries Without Bitterness

I told them something I wish someone had told me 20 years ago:

"Boundaries are not walls to keep people out.

They are doors gently letting love in and out without destroying the house they protect."

Boundaries don't say:

✕ "I don't love you."

They say:

✓ "I love you, but I love myself too."

Boundaries aren't punishment.

They are clarity.

They teach others what love can look like without sacrifice being the only language.

What We Wish Our Children Understood

"We are not here to rescue you every time life hurts.

We are here to love you while you learn to rescue yourself."

"We are not bottomless wells. We need pouring into too."

"And if we say 'no' it isn't rejection. It's survival."

Conversation at the Table

Lynn: "So how do we start?"

Me: "You start small. The first boundary is a whisper, not a scream."

Monica: "What does that sound like?"

Me: "It sounds like:
• 'I love you, but I can't today.'
• 'I want to help, but I need rest first.'
• 'I trust that you can handle this and I'm still here if you need guidance.'"

Sandra: "And what if they get mad?"

Me: "Then they get mad. Emotions won't kill them. But enabling might."

Take a deep breath and write honestly:

What is one boundary I need to set with someone I love?

What am I afraid will happen if I do?

Would I rather disappoint someone else or abandon myself again?

How would love feel if it didn't drain me?

Affirmations

My love is strong, but it no longer requires my suffering.

I can care without carrying.

I honor the woman I was and protect the woman I am becoming.

Saying "no" is an act of wisdom, not betrayal.

I deserve peace, even if they don't understand it yet.

The Kind of Love That Doesn't Hurt to Give

Evening light slid across the kitchen floor, touching the edge of the table where our hands rested. No one rushed to leave. No one looked at the clock. Because this; this honesty, this quiet safety was rare.

For once, we were not the ones fixing, listening, or saving everyone else.

We were the ones being seen.

The Words Around the Table

Sandra (softly): "So we're not selfish for being tired?"

Me: "No, baby. You're human."

Lynn: "And we don't have to keep proving we're good mothers?"

Me: "You already did. With every sacrifice no one saw. With every night you stayed up praying. You don't have to earn the right to rest."

Monica: "What if our kids never understand why we're changing?"

Me (gently): "Then let them misunderstand you for a season. One day, they might understand. And if they don't? You'll still have your peace. And that is not selfish that is survival."

Sandra (softly): "So we're not selfish for being tired?"

Me: "No, baby. You're human."

Lynn: "And we don't have to keep proving we're good mothers?"

Me: "You already did. With every sacrifice no one saw. With every night you stayed up praying. You don't have to earn the right to rest."

Monica: "What if our kids never understand why we're changing?"

Me (gently): "Then let them misunderstand you for a season. One day, they might understand. And if they don't? You'll still have your peace. And that is not selfish that is survival."

Write what your heart whispers but your mouth never says:

What do I need that I haven't forgiven myself for needing?

Where have I confused love with responsibility?

If I loved myself the way I love my children, what would I allow?

 What would I stop?

What would it look like if I trusted my children to take care of themselves?

Affirmations to Carry Into Tomorrow

I was never meant to be the hero of everyone's story.

My love does not require exhaustion to be real.

I can support without surrendering myself.

I am not stepping away from love; I'm stepping back into myself.

My boundaries are not rejection, they are protection.

As the night settled and the teacups emptied, I said the next truth we needed to face:

"In the next conversation, we need to talk about family; sisters, brothers, cousins, even our own mothers. The ones who say we've changed.

The ones who call us cold when we finally choose peace. Because love inside the family… that's where the guilt runs the deepest."

And just like that, we turned the page.

Between "The Mother Wound" and "When Family Calls It Betrayal"

Before you turn the page, breathe.

You've spoken truths you weren't always allowed to say; about mothers who loved imperfectly, daughters who carried too much, and the ache that lingers between love and survival.

This is where we pause not to fix the past, but to feel it. To understand that the little girl who once sought approval is the same woman now learning to approve of herself.

Forgiveness is not forgetting.
It's remembering without reopening the wound.

So before you enter the next chapter; where family love will be tested and boundaries will tremble, whisper to yourself:

"I am allowed to honor where I came from and still walk my own way."

Chapter 3 – When Family Calls It Betrayal:
Boundaries, Blood & Breaking the Cycle

"Family Doesn't Walk Away"… But What If Staying Is Hurting You?

Our next conversation didn't start with laughter or soft memories.

It started with a sentence that sat heavy in the room, spoken by Lynn as she stared into her untouched cup of tea:

"It hurts more when it's your own family who makes you feel like the enemy."

Silence spread across the table.

Because we all knew exactly what she meant.

The Unspoken Rule in Families

We are taught from the time we are little girls that:

Family is everything.

You don't turn your back on blood.

You forgive, even when it hurts.

You stay quiet to keep the peace.

You don't embarrass the family with the truth.

But no one talks about what happens when keeping the family together means breaking yourself apart.

No one prepares you for the day your sister, your brother, your mother, or your own child says:

"You've changed."

"You think you're better than us."

"You forgot where you come from."

What they really mean is:

"You stopped letting us use you."

"You stopped showing up for your own mistreatment."

"You stopped carrying the weight we put on you."

Around the Table — The Conversation Unfolds

Sandra: "My sister told the whole family I abandoned her just because I said I couldn't take care of Mama by myself anymore. "Monica: "My brother only calls when he needs money. When I finally said no, he said I 'must've forgotten who helped me when I was little.'"

Lynn: "My mother told everyone at church I don't visit her because I'm too busy 'enjoying my life.' She never said I offered to take her to appointments; she just didn't want me to choose how I helped."

They all turned to me.

Monica whispered: "Why is it that when we set boundaries, family acts like we declared war?"

What I Told Them

I looked at them, women carrying history in their bones and said quietly:

"Because in some families, love was built on sacrifice, not respect."

"If you were the helper, the fixer, the peacekeeper, then your role became your worth. And the minute you try to step out of that role, they don't see your pain… they see rebellion."

"They call it betrayal when you call it healing."

The Truth Beneath Their Accusations

WHEN THEY SAY: "You've changed."

WHAT IT REALLY MEANS:

"You don't let us treat you the same way anymore."

WHEN THEY SAY: "You're selfish."

WHAT IT REALLY MEANS:

"You finally chose yourself instead of choosing us every time."

WHEN THEY SAY: "You're breaking this family apart."

WHAT IT REALLY MEANS:

"You're exposing what we have worked hard to ignore or hide."

WHEN THEY SAY: "You think you're better than us."

WHAT IT REALLY MEANS:

"You have boundaries now — and we're not used to them."

WHEN THEY SAY: "You walked away from your family."

WHAT IT REALLY MEANS:

"You stopped accepting disrespect and called it self-respect."

Reflection Question

Has someone in your family ever called your healing a betrayal?

How did it make you feel and what did you do with that pain?

"You Left Us When We Needed You Most"

No one moves on from family pain quickly. The hurt sits differently when it's blood. You can argue with friends and walk away. But when it's your mother, your sister, your brother, your own child those wounds don't bleed outside. They bleed quietly, inside.

Sandra looked at me and said, "It's one thing when friends misunderstand you. But when it's your own people your own last name it cuts somewhere deeper. Somewhere you didn't even know could hurt."

I nodded, because I knew this story too well.

"You Left Me To Handle Mama Alone"
Lynn took a slow breath before she spoke.
"You all know Mama's been sick for a while. And for years, I have been the one doctor visit, medication, bathing, cooking, cleaning, all of it. My brother lives twenty minutes away, but somehow he's always 'too busy.' My sister says she can't help because she 'isn't good with medical things.'"

We nodded. We knew the script.

"But two months ago," she continued, "I told them I needed a break. I asked if one of them could stay with Mama for one week so I could rest."

She looked down at her hands.

"They didn't offer help. They gave me guilt."

"What did they say?" I asked quietly.

She swallowed. "My brother said, 'So you're just going to abandon us? You want us to do everything now? You're selfish for walking away when things get hard.' My sister said, 'Mama would never have left us like this.'"

Her voice cracked. "I didn't leave because I stopped loving her. I stepped back because I was drowning. But the way they told it; o the rest of the family sounded like I ran away."

Why This Happens

I reached across the table.

"They're not mad because you walked away," I told her. "They're mad because your absence revealed their lack of effort."

When one person has carried the emotional or physical responsibilities in a family for years; caregiving, financial support, peacekeeping, the others become comfortable. Sometimes even entitled.

So when the strong one finally steps back…

They don't see your exhaustion.

They see their convenience disappearing.

And instead of stepping up, they attack the person who stepped out.

Because blame is easier than responsibility.

Around the Table

Sandra: "I took care of my father alone for three years. The day I asked my brothers for help, they said I was being dramatic. I never asked again."

Monica: "I told my family I couldn't host Thanksgiving this year; my daughter told people I 'don't care about tradition anymore.'"

Lynn: "It's like the minute you stop breaking yourself for them, you're the problem."

Me: "No. You are not the problem. You're just the first one to admit you're tired."

Reflections

Write these questions down, truthfully, without guilt:

Have I carried responsibilities that were never meant to be mine alone?

Who benefits from me never saying no?

What would happen if I stopped doing everything? Would I lose their love or just their convenience?

If I keep going like this, what will it cost me; my health, my peace, my joy?

"You Think You're Better Than Us Now"

The air felt heavier as our conversation shifted. This wasn't about caregiving anymore. It wasn't about physical labor or financial help. It was about something quieter but sharper.

Jealousy. Comparison. Family pride.

Sometimes, the deepest wounds don't come from strangers or enemies. They come from people who share our blood but resent our healing.

"Oh, So You're Too Good for Us Now?"
Sandra sighed, then looked straight at me. "Can I tell you something I never wanted to admit?"
I nodded.
"After my divorce, I started healing slowly. I got into counseling. I joined a church group. I started saying no when things hurt me. I began to smile again, real smiles."
Her eyes softened.
"But instead of being happy for me, my own sister said, 'Ever since you got therapy and found Jesus, you act like you're better than us.'"
She swallowed.

"And my cousin told my daughter, 'Your mama forgot where she came from. She thinks she's too good for the family now that she's got a little peace.'"
The room fell silent.

Why This Happens

I reached over and touched her hand.
"They're not angry because you healed. They're angry because your healing reminds them they haven't."
When someone in the family grows, heals, or breaks a cycle:

They become a mirror.

That mirror forces others to see their pain, mistakes, or stagnation.

And if those people aren't ready to face that truth, they don't fix themselves; they attack the mirror.
Not because you're wrong.

But because your freedom exposes their cages.

Around the Table

Lynn: "My family said I changed when I stopped gossiping with them. I just didn't like talking about people anymore."

Monica: "When I started going to therapy, my brother said, 'We don't air family business to strangers. You're embarrassing us.'"

Sandra: "My mother said, 'Your grandma didn't need therapy. She prayed. You need to be strong like her.' But Grandma died with secrets she never healed from."

Me: "Survival is not the same as healing. Our mothers survived. But we are allowed to heal."

Reflections

Ask yourself gently:

Who in my family makes me feel guilty for growing?

Have I ever hidden my success, peace, or healing to make others comfortable?

What do I lose when I shrink myself to fit their expectations?

And what might I gain by continuing to grow; even if they don't clap for me?

What I Told Them

"Never apologize for healing," I said softly.

"If choosing peace makes you 'the villain,' then let them call you one. Knowing you chose peace is enough."

"You are not better than them. You are just no longer willing to stay broken to keep them comfortable."

Silent Jealousy, Sibling Resentment & Outgrowing Roles

Some wounds in families aren't caused by loud arguments; they're caused by quiet comparisons. By the glances. By the jokes meant to sting. By words like:

"Must be nice."
"Some of us don't have that luxury."
"You forgot where you came from."

They don't sound like hate.
They sound like hurt wearing pride.

When Success Became a Sin

Monica took a breath. "Can I tell you something I don't even say out loud at family gatherings?"

We nodded.

"You all know I went back to school in my 40s. Got my degree. Finally got the job I prayed for. I bought my first home at 52. I was proud… quietly proud."

"But at Thanksgiving, my brother said in front of everyone, 'Look at Miss Degree. Fancy house. I guess some of us weren't meant to be average.'"

Her voice softened.

"They laughed like it was a joke. But it wasn't. It was a reminder; Don't forget your place."

"And my sister hugged me after and whispered, 'We're happy for you… but don't act like you're above us now.'"

Why Family Resents Your Healing or Success
I looked at her with knowing eyes.

"Sometimes your growth confronts their comfort," I said.

"Your healing confronts their denial. Your success confronts their excuses."

And the truth is; jealousy in families often doesn't sound like jealousy. It sounds like judgment.

Not because they hate you.
But because your courage to become more reminds them of the parts of themselves they abandoned.

Friend to Friend — Around the Table

Lynn: "In my family, I was always the helper. When I stopped being available for every crisis… suddenly I was called 'different.'"

Sandra: "They loved me as long as I stayed the same version of myself they were comfortable with."

Me: "Families don't always hate your growth; they just miss the version of you who needed them more than you needed peace."

Quiet Truth You Spoke to Them

"It's okay to outgrow the role they gave you."
"It's okay if your healing makes some people uncomfortable."
"You are not responsible for shrinking yourself, so others won't feel small."

Write these down with honesty, not shame:

What role did my family give me? (Peacemaker, caretaker, provider, secret keeper, strong one).

What happens when I stop playing that role?

Who gets upset?

Why?

Do I dim my light to keep others comfortable? Where and with whom?

What would it feel like to show up as the real me; not the version of me they expect?

Affirmations — For When Family Doesn't Understand

I am allowed to grow, even if they preferred me small.

I can love my family and still choose myself.

My healing is not betrayal.

I am not better than them; I am simply becoming myself.

Blood is not a ticket to limitless access.

I can honor where I came from and still move forward.

"I Chose Distance, and They Called It Disrespect"

There comes a moment in every woman's life, especially in ours, now grandmothers, now tired in new ways; when love and survival no longer sit on the same side of the table.

Not because love is gone.
But because love, when it is taken for granted, begins to feel like injury.

"You Don't Come Around Anymore"
Lynn spoke quietly, like saying it too loudly would bring the pain back.

"My oldest sister called me last month and said, 'You don't come around anymore. You don't call like you used to. Ever since you got your own peace, you don't care about family.'"

She looked at her hands.
"What she didn't say was that every time I did show up; I left with less of myself. That every visit turned into another argument about how I 'changed.' Every conversation was a reminder of who they expected me to be."

She took a shaky breath.

"So I stopped staying long.
Stopped explaining myself.
Stopped bleeding in places that never tried to heal me."

"And now," she whispered, "they say I've abandoned them. They don't see I'm just trying not to abandon myself."

What I Told Her

I looked at her and said:

"Some people only love you when you're tired, available, and easy to use."

"The moment you get better, quieter, healthier, distant, they call it disrespect."

"But distance is not disrespect.
It is dignity with space around it."

She cried, the kind of tears that don't need sound.

Why Family Sees Boundaries as Betrayal

Because in many families, love is tied to access.

If you loved us, you'd always show up.
If you loved us, you'd sacrifice like we did.
If you loved us, you wouldn't need space.

But here's the truth I told them, and I'll tell anyone reading this:

Love without boundaries becomes bondage.
Loyalty without choice becomes slavery.

You can love them deeply and still choose distance.
You can pray for them and still protect your peace.
You can honor your family and still refuse to be their emotional punching bag.

Around the Table

Sandra: "I thought if I stepped back, they'd fall apart."
Monica: "They didn't fall apart; hey just found someone else to lean on."
Lynn: "Did I fail them?"
Me: "No, baby. You finally saved yourself."

Write what your heart needs, not what guilt tells you:
Who in my family drains me more than they love me?

What parts of myself shrink when I am around them?

What would it look like to love them from a healthy distance?

Am I willing to lose my peace, so I won't lose their approval?

Affirmations — When Family Doesn't Understand Your Healing

I can love people best when I am not losing myself to keep them comfortable.

Distance does not make me disloyal. It makes me honest.

I am not abandoning my family. I am returning to myself.

My peace is not a betrayal.

I choose love. But I do not choose harm.

Loving Them… Without Losing Yourself

The room had grown quiet in a peaceful kind of way. Not the silence of tension, but the kind that comes when truth has finally been spoken not to start a fight, but to free the heart.

Sandra leaned back in her chair and said softly, "So this is what it feels like… to say the truth out loud and not be ashamed of it."

I smiled at her that gentle, knowing smile only another woman who has survived love, motherhood, aging, and disappointment can offer.

Around the Table

Monica: "Do you think they'll ever understand us?"

Me: "Maybe. One day. Maybe not. But understanding isn't what we're living for now. We're living for peace."

Lynn: "Do you think setting boundaries means giving up on family?"

Me: "No. It means giving up on the belief that love only exists when we're suffering."

Sandra: "So we can love them… and still choose us?"

Me: "Yes. In fact, that's the only way love stays pure, when it isn't born from guilt, fear, or exhaustion."

They didn't say anything after that. But the way they breathed deeper told me they heard it.

Thoughts of Wisdom
I looked at my friends and said:

"You are not betraying your family by refusing to betray yourself."

"Your healing is not an attack on anyone; it is a homecoming to yourself."

"Some people may never clap for you, never apologize, never understand why you changed.
But your peace is not a group decision. It is yours to claim."

And with that, they smiled at me, a smile that said, Thank you for saying what we've been afraid to admit.

Write honestly, this page is for you:

Where have I confused loyalty with self-
abandonment?

Who do I shrink around to be accepted?

What is one boundary I need to set; not to hurt them,
but to protect me?

If peace was not selfish, what would I choose?

Affirmations

I can love them and still choose me.

My family's discomfort does not mean I am wrong.

I am not the villain for wanting peace.

I am allowed to grow beyond the role I was given.

My healing is not betrayal; it is bravery.

Between "When Family Calls It Betrayal" and "The Weight of Misunderstanding"

You told the truth this time.

You admitted that loving your family sometimes meant losing yourself and that choosing yourself was not betrayal, but bravery.

You stood up for your peace and called it sacred.

You saw how guilt hides behind loyalty and how silence can break cycles better than another apology ever could.

Take this moment before you move forward, close your eyes, breathe deeply, and feel the strength it took to get here.

You've set boundaries that your younger self never could.

You've learned that love doesn't have to look like pain to be real.

"Peace is not found in their understanding; it's found in your decision to stop explaining."

Carry that truth with you.

The next chapter will not ask you to fight harder; it will ask you to speak less, feel deeper, and protect your peace louder.

Chapter 4 – The Weight of Misunderstanding

When They Don't See Your Heart — Only Their Hurt

The next time we gathered, the air in the room felt gentler, not heavy, just thoughtful. The kind of quiet that follows truth. The kind that asks for more honesty, not more words.

Lynn was the first to speak this time. Her hands rested in her lap, the tea before her still untouched.

She said softly, "It's strange. You can spend your whole life loving people, doing everything you can for them… and the moment you do something for yourself, they look at you like you've turned into a stranger."

Sandra nodded, her eyes distant. "They say, 'You've changed,' like it's a bad thing."

Monica sighed. "My son told me last week, 'You're not the same mom you used to be.' He's right. I'm not. And yet somehow, that's what hurts the most."

I looked at them and said gently, "They don't mean you've changed. They mean they can't use you the same way anymore."

The room went still. We all knew that truth.

When They Rewrite Your Story

It's painful to be misunderstood by strangers.

But to be misunderstood by the ones you've loved, raised, and carried that's a deeper kind of ache.

You start to realize that sometimes people don't see you.

They see their memory of you, the one who never said no, never had limits, never asked for anything back.

So when you grow, they grieve that version of you.

Not because she was better, but because she made their lives easier.

"I told my daughter I was taking a few days to myself," Sandra said softly. "And she told me, 'You must be tired of us.' I wanted to tell her no, baby, I'm tired for me. But she wouldn't have heard it."

I nodded. "They hear through their hurt. Not your heart."

That's what misunderstanding does; it turns love into a translation problem.
You speak truth, but they only hear rejection.
You set boundaries, and they only feel abandonment.
You choose peace, and they only see pride.

"You Don't Call Like You Used To"
Monica looked down. "My daughter said that to me last week. 'You don't call like you used to.'"
She laughed quietly not out of humor, but exhaustion.

"I told her, 'I still love you the same. I'm just not chasing conversations that only drain me.' She didn't understand. She thought I was pulling away."

She took a deep breath.
"I wanted to say baby, I stopped calling every day because every call became about what I could fix. Not how I was doing. And I just needed someone to ask about me for once."

I reached across the table. "Sometimes silence isn't distance, it's self-preservation."

The room fell quiet again.

Because every woman at that table knew what it felt like to stop explaining herself just to survive another misunderstanding.

Why They Don't Understand

I said softly, "It's not that they don't love us. It's that they love the version of us who made their lives easier. Growth threatens the comfort of people who've never had to question the roles we played."

Lynn wiped a tear. "So no matter how much I explain myself, they'll still see me through their pain?"

"Yes," I said. "Because understanding requires humility and not everyone's ready for that."

Misunderstanding is what happens when love refuses to evolve. It's when they want the same you, even though you're no longer the same woman.

You can't shrink back to make them comfortable. You can't stop growing to stay familiar. And you can't keep explaining peace to people who've mistaken chaos for love.

Around the Table

Sandra: "They don't see I'm just trying to breathe."

Monica: "They call it pride. I call it peace."

Lynn: "They say I've changed. But what if changing was the only way I could keep living?"

Me: "Then change, baby. Let them call it what they want. You know the truth."

When You Stop Explaining Yourself

At some point, we stop defending our peace.

Not out of anger; but out of wisdom.

You realize that explanation is a love language meant
for people who want to understand you.
If they're determined to misunderstand, your silence
will speak clearer than any paragraph ever could.

"Sometimes," I said, "silence is not the absence of love;
it's the refusal to keep begging to be seen."

No one argued.
They just sipped their tea, letting that truth sink in the
way only women who've lived it can.

Reflection

Write this down and answer gently, without guilt:

Who keeps misunderstanding my growth as distance?

Have I been trying to explain my peace to people committed to their chaos?

What would happen if I stopped explaining and simply started living?

Can I still love them, even if they never understand me?

Affirmations — For When They Don't See Your Heart

I no longer explain my peace to those who prefer my pain.

Their misunderstanding of me is not my responsibility.

My silence is strength, not surrender.

I can love them from afar and still wish them well.

I am not cold; I am healing in quiet places they cannot see.

When Silence Protects You

When Speaking Drains You More Than Staying Quiet

The night had grown still, but none of us moved.

There's a kind of silence that doesn't feel empty; it feels earned.

It was that kind of silence now.

Sandra finally broke it, her voice low but steady.

"You ever get tired of explaining yourself to people who don't want to hear you?"

We all nodded. Because we knew.

Lynn added softly, "Sometimes I think the only peace I'll ever get is in the quiet; when nobody's asking me to defend why I need it."

The room went still again.

Not from tension, but from recognition.

We've spent a lifetime explaining our hearts to people who only listen for what offends them.

When Words Become Too Heavy

There comes a point when words don't heal anymore, they reopen.

You try to explain your pain to people who only want to be right.

You try to explain your boundaries to those who've benefited from your lack of them.

And little by little, you realize that peace doesn't need to be explained; it needs to be lived.

"I stopped trying to convince them," Monica said softly. "Every time I spoke my truth, they heard an attack. Every time I said I was tired, they heard rejection. So now I just say less."

Sandra nodded. "That's not giving up. That's protecting your heart."

"You Don't Talk to Me Like You Used To"

Lynn looked down at her hands. "My sister said that to me last month. She said, 'You don't talk to me like you used to.' And I wanted to tell her ; it's not that I don't want to talk. It's that talking hurts now."

Her voice softened. "Because every conversation turns into something I did wrong. Something I didn't do enough of. I got tired of defending a heart that only wanted peace."

I reached across and touched her hand. "Sometimes silence isn't distance, it's self-respect."

The Strength in Quiet

When we were younger, we thought strength meant speaking up.
Now we know, sometimes strength is what you don't say.
We learned that not every battle deserves our words.
That not every misunderstanding requires our voice.
That peace sometimes sounds like letting people sit with the story they've written about you, while you quietly live the truth.

"People think silence means surrender," I said. "But sometimes silence is the loudest boundary there is."

Monica smiled faintly. "Silence used to scare me. Now it feels like home."

What Silence Teaches You

When you stop explaining, something powerful happens.

You begin to hear your own thoughts again.

You begin to notice how often you used to apologize for feeling.

You begin to rest, not because everything is fixed, but because you're no longer trying to fix everyone else.

Sandra said softly, "I used to think silence meant bitterness. But now I know; it's just peace with less noise."

We all smiled. Because we knew exactly what she meant.

Around the Table

Lynn: "Silence is how I protect what's left of me."

Monica: "If peace requires explanation, it's not peace, it's performance."

Sandra: "Quiet doesn't mean I've stopped caring. It means I'm done pleading."

Me: "Yes. Silence isn't punishment. It's preservation."

Lynn: "Silence is how I protect what's left of me."

Monica: "If peace requires explanation, it's not peace, it's performance."

Sandra: "Quiet doesn't mean I've stopped caring. It means I'm done pleading."

Me: "Yes. Silence isn't punishment. It's preservation."

Affirmations — When Silence Feels Lonely

My silence is not weakness. It is wisdom.

I do not owe explanations to those committed to misunderstanding me.

Quiet doesn't mean I've stopped loving; it means I'm learning to love myself too.

Peace does not shout. It simply stays.

I am not disappearing; I am healing in places words can't reach.

The Peace That Doesn't Need to Be Proven

When You No Longer Defend the Life That Heals You

The teapot had gone cold hours ago. The candles burned low, small halos of light dancing across our faces. But no one moved.

Some conversations don't end because they're finished, they end because peace has entered the room.

Monica leaned back in her chair, staring at nothing in particular. "You know what I realized tonight?" she said. "All this time, I've been trying to prove that I'm still a good daughter, a good mother, a good woman, even after I started saying no."

Sandra tilted her head. "And did it work?"

Monica smiled faintly. "No. The more I tried to prove myself, the more they expected me to keep earning their love."

Her voice broke a little. "But love isn't something we should have to earn, is it?"

I shook my head. "No, baby. Real love doesn't come with a receipt."

When Peace Stops Seeking Permission

There comes a point when you stop defending your peace, not out of pride, but out of understanding.

You realize you don't need to explain the life that finally lets you breathe.

Lynn spoke next. "I used to think I had to convince them that I wasn't angry. That I wasn't walking away, just walking differently. But they never heard me."

I looked at her and said gently, "Because they can't hear peace if they're still addicted to your chaos."

She nodded slowly. "Then I guess I've made peace with being misunderstood."

Sandra smiled softly. "That's the kind of peace that doesn't ask for permission."

"You Don't Care Anymore"

Sandra looked down, tracing her finger along the rim of her cup. "My son told me that last month. 'You don't care anymore.'"

She paused, her voice trembling. "And for a moment, I almost believed him. Until I realized, I do care. I just care differently now. I care without losing myself."

The room fell silent again.

Because every woman there had been accused of not caring, when all she wanted was to be cared for, too.

I said softly, "When you stop rescuing people from their own lessons, they'll always call it neglect."

When You Choose Quiet Joy

Peace changes your appetite.

You no longer crave validation; you crave quiet mornings.

You no longer need everyone's approval, you just need your spirit to stop feeling heavy.

Monica said, "It's strange. I thought healing would make me louder, more confident. But instead, it made me quieter. Softer. Still."

I smiled at her. "That's how you know it's real. Peace doesn't shout. It settles."

Lynn added, "I used to pray for everyone to understand me. Now I just pray for peace to stay."

Sandra whispered, "Maybe that's what growing up really is realizing you don't need applause to feel seen."

Around the Table

Monica: "Peace doesn't ask for witnesses. It just wants room."

Lynn: "If I have to explain my healing, it's not healing, it's performance."

Sandra: "I don't need them to clap. I just need to keep breathing."

Me: "Yes. Because the peace you protect will one day protect you."

No one said another word after that.

The quiet that followed wasn't awkward, it was holy.

A silence stitched together by grace, wisdom, and release.

Reflections

Find a quiet space before you answer. Let your heart whisper, not your guilt:

Where in my life am I still trying to prove my worth to people who don't see me?

What would it look like to stop defending my peace and start living it?

Who still mistakes my silence for distance instead of growth?

What does peace mean to me, in this season of my life?

Affirmations — When Peace Finally Finds You

I no longer chase understanding. I choose peace.

My joy doesn't need validation to be real.

Being misunderstood no longer breaks me, it frees
me.

I am proud of the woman I've become, even if they
can't see her clearly.

Peace is not a place I found; it's who I've become.

Before "Letting Go of Their Version of You"

This chapter taught you something sacred, that peace doesn't need proof, silence can be holy, and being misunderstood is not failure.

You no longer chase understanding from those who never tried to listen.
You no longer beg for grace from those who misuse it.
You've realized that being called "different," "selfish," or "changed" was never an insult; it was confirmation that healing is working.

Now, as you step into the next chapter, know this:
You don't have to live in the versions of yourself they remember.
You are free to become the woman you've prayed to meet.
"I am not who they say I am.
I am who peace has made me."

Let this page be your quiet declaration.
The next part of your story isn't about proving; it's about becoming.

Chapter 5 – Letting Go of Their Version of You

"I Am No Longer Who They Needed Me To Be,

I Am Who I Needed To Become"

We didn't rush that evening. We didn't talk fast or fill silence.

Healing has its own pace, and it rarely moves in a straight line.

Sandra sat quietly, fingers lightly resting on her teacup. "I spent most of my life trying to live up to a picture they painted of me," she said softly. "The dependable one. The strong one. The one who never broke."

She looked up then, with eyes tired but clear.
"But I realize something now. I wasn't strong; I was silent."

None of us spoke at first. We just nodded, because we had lived that sentence too.

When They Loved The Version You Outgrew

Lynn exhaled slowly.

"It's painful," she whispered, "when they mourn the version of you that made them comfortable."

Monica sighed. "They liked me better when I didn't know myself. When I didn't speak up. When I said 'yes' to things that hurt me."

"That wasn't love," I murmured.

"That was convenience dressed as affection."

They all looked at me, waiting.

"We were never villains," I said. "We were women who finally stopped shrinking."

And for the first time in a long time, we didn't defend that truth. We simply let it rest in the air.

Releasing the Weight of Expectation

"I always thought I owed them the version of me they were used to," Sandra whispered.

"But the truth is... I only owed God the chance to see who I could become."

If you have ever rebuilt yourself, piece by trembling piece, you know the quiet courage it demands.

You know the moment when you stop apologizing for who you are.
For what you want.
For what you had to leave behind to breathe.

Letting go of their version of you isn't abandonment,
it is homecoming.

"I Miss Who You Used to Be"

Monica brushed a tear away.

"My sister said that to me. 'I miss who you used to be.'"

She smiled, but it wasn't joy, it was truth turned into strength.

"I wanted to say, I do too. But she was tired. She was hurting. She was obedient to everyone but herself."

Silence settled again.

Healing often sounds like silence, not because there's nothing to say, but because the heart is learning to breathe without asking permission.

Around the Table

Lynn: "I release who they think I should be."

Sandra: "I honor who I am becoming."

Monica: "I am no longer defined by the version they preferred."

Me: "Peace arrives the moment you stop auditioning for love."

Reflections

Answer softly, there is no rush, no judgment, only truth:

Whose expectations am I still holding onto?

Where in my life do I still shrink to avoid disappointment?

What part of myself am I finally ready to reclaim?

Who am I becoming when no one is watching?

Affirmations — Releasing Their Version of Me

I honor my growth, even if they prefer my past.

I am not obligated to stay where I hurt.

I do not need permission to evolve.

I release the roles that kept me small.

I am becoming the woman I prayed for.

Chapter 6 – The Peaceful Woman They Called the Villain

"I Was Never the Villain — I Was the Woman Who Finally Chose Peace"

The rain had started sometime during our talk, soft at first, then steady, like heaven's way of washing away what no longer needed to stay.

We sat together in the glow of the last candle, the four of us, older now, wiser, still carrying pieces of the women we once were.

No one rushed to leave.

Because some nights aren't about finishing, they're about remembering how far you've come.

Sandra spoke first.

"I used to want them to see me," she said softly. "To understand that I wasn't trying to be difficult. I was just tired of being invisible."

Lynn nodded. "And now?"

Sandra smiled. "Now I just want peace. Whether they see it or not."

We all smiled at that.
Because that's where every story in this room had been heading, not toward revenge or regret, but toward quiet freedom.

When Peace Becomes the Point
Monica leaned forward, her voice tender.
"I think that's what they never understood. We weren't trying to fight anyone. We were just trying to stop fighting ourselves."

I looked at her and said, "That's the difference between bitterness and healing. Bitterness wants them to hurt. Healing just wants peace."

The room went quiet again.
You could hear the rain tapping against the window, slow, forgiving.

Maybe this is what peace really feels like:
No need to prove, no need to plead, no need to explain.
Just stillness; the kind that says, I made it through.

The Story They'll Tell vs. The Truth You'll Live

Lynn exhaled deeply. "They'll probably always call me stubborn, maybe even selfish."

Monica nodded. "They'll say I changed."

Sandra added, "They'll say I pulled away."

I smiled, warm and steady. "And they'll be right; but not in the way they mean. You did change. You did pull away. But you did it to find peace. And there's no villain in that story, only a woman who finally chose herself."

We let that truth linger, because it felt like the kind of ending that doesn't need applause. Just understanding.

"You Seem Happier Now"

Sandra laughed lightly. "My granddaughter told me that last week. 'Grandma, you seem happier now.' And I told her, 'That's because I finally stopped explaining myself to people who never really listened.'"

We laughed with her, not out of humor, but relief. Because sometimes joy isn't loud, it's quiet, steady, and unbothered.

Around the Table

Lynn: "Maybe we weren't the villains. Maybe we were the ones who broke the pattern."
Monica: "Maybe peace looks selfish when you've only known sacrifice."
Sandra: "Maybe healing doesn't need witnesses, only courage."
Me: "Maybe the truest peace comes when you stop waiting for an apology and start giving yourself permission to rest."

The rain slowed. The candles flickered low.
We didn't need to say more.
Our stories had spoken for us.

A Gentle Goodbye

When it was time to go, we didn't hug in a rush. We held one another the way women do when they know the power of surviving.

Sandra whispered, "Thank you; for helping me see I wasn't wrong for changing."
Lynn said, "For the first time, I'm proud of my peace."

Monica smiled through tears. "Maybe being called the villain wasn't punishment. Maybe it was protection."

And I told them, "You were never the villain, baby. You were the woman who finally told the truth, and peace came because of it."

Reflections

Find a quiet corner before you write and let peace
answer for you:

What story about me am I ready to rewrite?

Where have I confused being good with being silent?

What does peace look like in my own life, not
borrowed, but mine?

Can I accept being misunderstood if it means being
free?

Affirmations – Living As the Peaceful Woman

I am no longer at war with myself.

I can love them — and still choose me.

My peace is not rebellion; it is restoration.

I no longer chase understanding, I live truth.

They called me the villain, but peace called me home.

To the Woman Reading This

You were never wrong for wanting peace.

You were never difficult for setting boundaries.

You were never heartless for walking away from chaos.

You are simply the woman who remembered her worth.

And when they call you the villain, smile gently, because peace is misunderstood by those still living in turmoil.

"You are not who they said you were.

You are who you decided to become."

Close this book knowing:

You didn't just read a story; you became part of one.

A story of women who stopped apologizing for being whole.

And that, my friend,

is the most beautiful ending of all.

To the Woman Who Was Called the Villain

You were never the villain.

You were the woman who finally decided her peace mattered.

You stopped begging for permission to exist whole.

You stopped explaining the boundaries that protect your heart.

You stopped trying to heal people who refused to stop hurting you.

They called it selfish.

They called it pride.

They called it betrayal.

But you know what it really was?

It was freedom.

It was the moment you remembered that you are not required to stay small so others can stay comfortable.

It was the season you stopped carrying everyone else's storm and started walking toward your own sunlight.

You outgrew the guilt that used to hold you hostage.

You learned that forgiveness doesn't always mean reunion.

And you finally made peace with being misunderstood, because peace was the only understanding you needed.

So if they never apologize…

If they never understand your healing…

If they still tell stories that paint you as the one who "changed"…let them.

You have nothing left to prove.

You are not the villain.

You are the lesson.

The boundary.

The answered prayer for the woman you used to be.

May you move forward knowing that peace was never a punishment, it was a homecoming.

And may you always remember:

Your strength is not loud.

Your softness is not weakness.

Your story is not over, it's just yours now.

"You were never too much.

You were simply too free."

With grace and understanding,

— Vgdawson

Helpful Resources

For the woman learning to choose peace without guilt

A Gentle Word Before You Begin

My friend, if you've made it this far, I want you to know something:

You are not broken.
You are not too late.
And you are not alone.

Sometimes, we need a little more support beyond conversations like this, someone to talk to, something to read, a place to go when the weight feels too heavy.

These resources are here to support your healing, not replace your strength.

Take what you need. Leave what you don't.

Emotional & Mental Health Support

There is no shame in needing someone to talk to. In fact, it is one of the strongest things you can do.

- National Alliance on Mental Illness (NAMI)
  Offers education, support groups, and resources for emotional well-being. Sometimes, just hearing "me too" from someone else can bring relief.

- Mental Health America
  Provides free mental health screenings and

information on stress, anxiety, and emotional exhaustion.

- Substance Abuse and Mental Health Services Administration
A confidential, free helpline (1-800-662-HELP) if you feel overwhelmed and need immediate support.

Healing Practices for Everyday Peace

You don't always need a big solution. Sometimes you need small, quiet moments that bring you back to yourself.

- Journaling:
Write what you couldn't say out loud. Be honest. This is your safe place.

- Quiet Time (Even 10 Minutes):
Sit without noise, without demands. Just breathe.

- Walking:
Not for exercise — for release. Let your thoughts move through you.

- Prayer or Meditation:
However you speak to God, or your inner peace keep that connection sacred.

Books That Speak to the Same Journey

If you're looking for deeper understanding, these books may support you:

- Boundaries
  A powerful guide to learning when to say yes and when to say no.

- Set Boundaries, Find Peace
  Clear, practical advice for protecting your peace without guilt.

- The Gifts of Imperfection
  A reminder that you are already enough without over giving or overproving.

Community & Support Circles

Healing becomes easier when you are not doing it alone.

- Local church groups or women's circles

- Senior or grandmother support groups

- Online communities focused on boundaries, healing, and personal growth

Sometimes, just sitting in a room where someone understands your story can change everything.

When You Need Immediate Support

If you are feeling overwhelmed, deeply discouraged, or emotionally drained:

- 988 Suicide and Crisis Lifeline — Dial or text 988 (available 24/7)
  You don't have to be in crisis to call. You just have to need someone to listen.

Final Words from Me to You

My friend…

You have spent a lifetime being strong for everyone else.

Now it is time to be gentle with yourself.

You don't need to fix everything today.

You don't need to explain yourself to everyone.

Just take one step:

One boundary

One honest thought

One moment of peace

And let that be enough for today.

**You are not the villain.
You are the woman who finally chose herself and
that is something to be proud of.**

Stay Connected

Stay inspired between books and join our growing circle of women choosing peace, purpose, and truth.

Website: www.what2buynext.com
Instagram: @what2buynext
TikTok: @what2buynext
Etsy: what2buynext Bookshelf

For book updates, speaking requests, and literary candle collections, visit the website and subscribe to the newsletter for reflections, behind-the-scenes updates, and new releases.

Thank You Page

Dear Reader,

Thank you for sitting at this table with us, for listening, reflecting, and letting these words meet you where you are.

You didn't just read this book, you shared space with stories that mirror your strength, your resilience, and your capacity to love again.

If these pages brought you comfort, healing, or peace, I hope you'll carry that energy into your next season. Tell another woman she's not alone. Remind her she's not the villain for wanting peace.

Every book I write is a conversation and this one wouldn't be complete without you.

With gratitude,

— *Vgdawson*

 May your peace be loud enough to silence every false story ever told about you.